GW00367978

OUR G

LIFE-STORIES

Brian Grogan, S.J.

A Book for Personal and Group Development

What God is Making of Us All

Messenger Publications

Published by
Messenger Publications,
37, Lower Leeson Street,
Dublin 2
Tel: 353 1 6767491/2
Fax 353 1 6611606

Copyright © 2000 Messenger Publications.

ISBN 1 872245 56 0

Nihil Obstat: **Tim Hamilton, S.J.,**
                         Censor Deput.

Imprimi Potest: **+Desmond,**
                         Archbishop of Dublin.
                         3rd December 1999

Printed by Grafton Litho Ltd, Hanover St., Dublin 2.

Contents

Introduction

'Not another book on Grace!'

Yes! Let's admit that a vast number of books on grace already exist. Most of them are unread and unknown. By this I mean not only that there are books about grace gathering dust on shelves, but rather that each of us is a book telling the story of grace, but we do not know this. Yes, your story is a graced one, as is everybody else's. What I hope to do is to help you open your book, turn the pages, identify the main themes and the central characters, and ponder how to construct the chapters of your life still to come.

Yours is a unique story, a first edition. It is as yet far from complete - there are lots of blank pages! You may consider that the tale so far is pretty ordinary and commonplace, hardly a best-seller. Your image of yourself may be of someone who plods along quietly and dully, alone and unimportant, and that no intelligent publisher would want your manuscript, were you to submit it.

But when you catch on to the fact that the text is co-authored, everything changes. You look back on the story thus far with a new interest, to see what the ghost-writer (God!) has been up to. You begin to see that the story-line is incredibly rich - no trivial paperback this, but something that has the makings of a minor saga. You catch on to the amazing fact that everyone else's story is also being co-authored, and you get excited as you begin to puzzle out how all the stories fit together in what can only be intended as a cosmic epic.

You now begin to get into the habit of consulting with your ghost-writer on how best to construct the next chapter. You find yourself noticing how incidents on earlier pages, which appeared up to now to be bare facts without much relevance, are now assuming greater importance. It's a bit like a good detective novel, in which casual hints in the early pages turn out to be decisive at the end. Everything begins to hang together: nothing is unimportant. Every detail has its own richness in the total plot. The fascination in working along with an open storyline, where you and the other characters are free to choose which way to go, is endless. So too is the mystery of how the ghost-writer will make sense of all the individual contributions.

As you look further ahead you come to see that the final chapter will be written posthumously, not by you but entirely by the ghost-writer. Yet it won't be simply an epitaph, a summing up and conclusion, with no more to be said. No, it will be more like the introduction to a new volume in which your life really gets going. The scenario will be unimaginably exciting, and the relationships totally satisfying. In the meantime, you find that you've a greater interest in the stories of others, and you hope and pray that unlike human epics in which some achieve victory at the expense of others, the final triumph of the cosmic epic will be shared by all, with all characters safely home and all enmities reconciled. Only then, you feel, can the great feast begin!

This little book, then, offers hints and illustrations which may help you catch on to your story of Grace. Grace is a compact word which can be decoded in many ways, but the simplest way to think of Grace is as 'God's help'. Your story of Grace is the account of

2

the limitless ways in which God has helped, is help-ing, and will help you to become like Godself. Through good events God helps you to move along smoothly towards that goal: with bad events God has to wrestle, often mightily, to turn them to your good.

Suggestions For Group Use

While this book will help your private reading and reflection, it is also designed for group work. The health of the Church depends largely on the life, ener-gy and vision found in small groups. There are, thank God, innumerable Christian groups working away at this present time, but all need steady nourishing, else they will run dry. When groups founder it is not that their task has become irrelevant, but often that they lose sight of their vision. 'Unless the people have vision, they perish!' (Proverbs 29:18). To avoid becoming spent, burnt-out, a group must renew its vision and re-find its place in the wide scheme of God's projects and dreams for the world.

This book is designed for such busy groups, to enrich their vision and give them an injection of hope and energy. It will also give them a deep reverence and respect for everyone they work with.

There are 12 chapters, so the book can be covered in a year. It can be used as follows.

1. The members agree to read a chapter privately between meetings: this can be done comfortably in about 30 minutes. They then pray through the Suggested Prayer, and mull over the topic For Pondering in odd moments. It helps also to chat it out with a friend, because, as someone said, we all have one wing, and we need to connect up with someone else in order to fly!

2. The group meeting begins with the Suggested Prayer exercise, and is followed by sharing on the content of the chapter, for an agreed time, depending on what business has to be dealt with at the meeting. Try not to let the demands of the agenda eclipse the time needed to clarify your vision!

Make sure everyone has a chance to share, even briefly. Don't look so much for clear answers as for a deepening sense of reverence and awe at what God is doing. God delights in each member of the group, and is endlessly active in each one's life. Speak personally about what touched your heart. 'What struck me was...' 'I wonder if...' - such are good ways to explore the holy mystery which grace is. Wide-eyed wonder and glad surprise are the right attitudes as we discover something of the artistry involved in God's making each of us, and all of us together, 'God's work of art' (Eph 2:10).

This sensitivity will enable you to go about your apostolic work with ever greater delicacy, in the awareness that in dealing with another you are 'standing on holy ground' (Exod 3:5), for God is in that other person's life long before you came and will be there when you are gone. You will also have greater confidence in knowing that God is doing the main work and you are God's helper. 'It is God (not we!) who makes things grow' (1 Cor 3:7). Lastly, a main theme of these pages is that since God never despairs of any of us, neither should we. Everyone has their personal story of grace. Discover yours and you will help others to discover theirs!

Chapter One

What Is Grace?

Grace is an umbrella word which covers all that goes on between God and ourselves, so it is all about relationships. We will explore this relationship both from God's point of view, because grace comes from God, and from our own, because grace is at work everywhere in us and in our world. Grace is Love, God's love at work in our lives, helping us to become our full selves.

Let's start our exploration by using the individual letters of the word GRACE to create a rule of thumb definition of grace. Thus G = God; R = Reveals; A = And; C = Calls; E = Endlessly. Thus the word GRACE connotes 'God Reveals And Calls Endlessly'. Just now this decoding of 'GRACE' may not mean very much to you, but the depth of meaning in the five words will unfold through stories, explanations and exercises. The wonderful world of grace is waiting for you to explore it, no matter how difficult or bad life may be for you at present. There's a huge risk in believing that grace is for you, but I invite you to take that risk.

In a Nutshell

In a nutshell, what is grace about? It's all about relationships, as we said above. It's the wonder of being accepted for who you are; the unexpected and joyous surprise of being found lovable. This is not a pitying acceptance: it is the extraordinary fact that God thinks we're wonderful, and that God gazes on each one of us and smiles. I make God smile! God sees so much more in us than the world sees: God's gaze is a kindly one, with a limitless warmth that evokes the best in us. God's mood is always loving: it does not change as our moods do in regard to ourselves and others.

We're invited to take the risk of looking at ourselves from God's point of view as we've just described. We are asked to accept the invitation to respond to a relationship which from God's side is steady and eternally dependable. The harshness of life teaches us not to expect such unwavering graciousness from others. But that's precisely why the early Christians described this mysterious openheartedness of God as a free gift, translated in Latin as '*gratia*', from which we get the English word GRACE.

A child was asked, 'If God told you he loved you, what would you do?' 'I'd answer, I love you too!' 'And would you love yourself because God loves you?' 'Well, we're not meant to, but I think I would. But it would be a secret between us!'

Popular Usage

The word 'grace' has largely fallen out of favour nowadays. This is hardly surprising since it was often used to connote bartering between God and ourselves, which went like this:

> I did something good and God rewarded me; I did something bad and the all-seeing God, like a just but stern schoolteacher, punished me appropriately. Good was rewarded, badness was punished. We each had our own store of grace, rather like a private bank account: the balance rose or fell according to our actions. Confession on Saturday night cleared the debts and gave us a deposit of grace which gradually diminished during the week because of our failures and weaknesses. Mortal sin wiped it out completely. While the love of God was spoken of, it often seemed to be without a heart; a cold, calculating and cautious 'love': we earned our way to heaven.

Somebody reminded me recently of her `arrangement' with God by which she felt that she could have a good time on Friday night because she'd be going to confession on Saturday! She admitted that she often was afraid that she'd die on Friday night: that God would 'get' her before she 'got' confession.

So much for the bartering arrangement: it was a very inadequate way of understanding the loving relationship between God and ourselves, which the word grace enfolds. Bartering has no place in the world of grace where all is `free gift' and the giving of the gift does not depend on the goodness of the recipient.

A Gracious Attitude

Although the word 'grace' is largely out of favour today, it is still full of meaning. We've all met 'gracious' people, by which we mean that they have qualities of kindness, gentle tolerance, a smiling attitude. It's good to be in their company because they make us feel at ease in being who we are. Perhaps that's because they themselves are at ease with who they are.

Now apply all of this to God! God is the gracious person, kind, accepting, tolerant and smiling. Thus to meet God and develop a relationship with God is the most wonderful experience we can ever have.

Grace-filled Meals

We link the word grace with the simplest of all things - meals. When we say 'Grace' we ask a blessing on our food and then give thanks for it. By acknowledging and including God somehow this can change the atmosphere of the meal. The film, Babette's Feast, comes to mind: for Babette, preparing a meal was an act of love. For the guests, her graciousness was palpable. They were softened and more reverent towards one another, at least while they enjoyed the feast for which she happily gave everything she had.

Perhaps you are among the many people who spend a considerable portion of their lives preparing meals for others. It can help to recall that a meal can be a time of real grace, a gesture of love on the part of the cook which can bind together those who share what is prepared. A meal, however simple, is a symbol of how things are meant to be: the food and drink are ultimately the gift of a gracious and provident God who looks after us. The person who does the shopping and prepares the meal is given an opportunity to act on God's behalf, even in the choice of foods for particular tastes. When things are at their best, those at table are bonded together in harmony and friendship. Then a simple meal becomes a microcosm of the most gracious meal of all,the great feast being prepared for the close of human history. Then everyone will sit down together in mutual acceptance. The most wonderful of all hosts, the Three Divine Persons, will lead the celebration and beam delightedly on us all.

The Wash-up

But what about the wash-up? That task can also be a moment of grace. A mother told me that many good conversations happen at her sink. Washing up is humdrum work. It doesn't demand much attention, so people are free to talk in a relaxed atmosphere in which confidences may be shared. It's very different when people walk off and leave someone stranded at the sink. What happens to grace then? The image of the meal reveals the central truth about grace which recurs throughout these pages: GRACE IS ALL ABOUT RELATIONSHIPS. In its primary meaning, grace refers to the loving relationship which God is continually trying to develop with us: it then refers to loving relationships among ourselves. So when people who should help to clean up after a meal walk away, grace is thwarted because an opportunity for showing practical love is ignored.

To Summarise

Is the formula 'God Reveals And Calls Endlessly' beginning to unfold for you? Are you beginning to believe that the Three Divine Persons are constantly revealing Themselves as kind? Can you allow yourself to hear Their endless call to you? Are you ready to take a step in believing that They are always working to help you, that They labour so that the reality around you may be helpful to you? Can you risk trusting that They labour endlessly to undo the damage which others cause you, and which you also cause to others?

As we move on, we'll be talking about the reasons why each of us can take the risk of trusting God and living out our lives to the full. God is totally on our side, and especially in the 'valleys of darkness' that we go through (cf Psalm 23). No matter how disastrous, unpromising and unwieldy a situation may be, we can still hope because God will never give up on any of us.

Don't think of grace as weak and timid. Picture it as a love which though delicate and sensitive is so strong and muscular that it's able to carry out God's purposes beyond our hopes and dreams (cf Eph 3:20). If this is so, then we can be less fearful about letting God co-author our lives.

For Prayer

It's good to begin prayer by noticing how God or Jesus looks on you.

* Picture yourself coming upon Jesus as he sits alone, deep in thought. You make a sound -- he hears and turns his head towards you. Perhaps he lifts his hand to shield his eyes from the glare of the sun.

* Watch him as he recognises you. See the smile begin and then spread across his face.

* What goes on in you? Doubt, tears, relief, tentative hope, yearning .....

* Can you return the smile? Can you walk or hurry towards him?

* Let the scene unfold.

For Pondering

Can you identify people who have helped you believe that you are loved just as you are? Can you think also of people whom you have helped to believe in themselves as loved? How did it happen?

Chapter Two

Your Life-story Is Graced

In the first chapter we spoke about grace being present in two very simple and everyday events: in smiles and in meals. A smile reveals goodwill, openness and love: it is a first step in building relationships, which are what grace is all about.

A 17th century French mystic wrote at length about her experience of the relationship between God and herself, but she summed it up happily in a wonderful phrase: 'You gazed on me and you smiled.' This is an apt description of grace: God smiling on us endlessly, and all that that implies.

Smiles and Meals

We spoke too about meals as a sign of grace, because they build good relationships in the simplest possible way. Food and drink are gifts, and so is the love with which they are prepared. In the L'Arche communities founded by Jean Vanier to care for those with learning disabilities, meals are central: each one is a celebration of life and love and togetherness. Meals don't begin until everyone is present, and they begin with 'Grace'. Those getting the meals ready are asked to prepare the food with love: if they find that they're out of sorts they're asked to change with someone else! Would many a family go hungry if that were the arrangement in every home? The belief in the L'Arche communities is that those at table can tell by instinct whether the meal has been prepared graciously or not.

Smiles and meals are part of everyday life: they are precious moments of grace and God wants to be present in them as in all of our lives.

Your Story

Your whole life is a tapestry of grace, which means that God is present in and around every detail of it! Can you believe that? Try to, as we focus on your graced life-story. Keep in mind that grace connotes 'God Reveals And Calls Endlessly'. By looking at your life you can come to notice with happy surprise that God is constantly revealing Godself lovingly to you: God is truly involved with you, with those you love and (surprise!) those you have difficulty with. God is always taking initiatives that will be helpful to you, while leaving you free to decide what to do. God has been calling you from the beginning of your life, and will continue to call you through all events until you reach that fullness of life and joy with God which is your destiny. As you uncover this activity of God you can begin to understand that truly your life is full of grace.

A contemporary version of Gabriel's greeting to Mary (Luke 1:28) goes as follows: 'Good morning!

You are beautiful with God's beauty, beautiful inside and out! God be with you.' Try letting God whisper that greeting to you at the beginning of your day. It will give you encouragement to face the day's surprises with the confidence that God will always be around to help you.

Exploring

One way of exploring the presence of grace in your life is to begin chronologically, and to go through your life year by year or period by period. What are you looking out for? You're trying to notice where love in any of its many forms was present, because grace is love-in-action. Where was there care, understanding, sympathy, appreciation, tolerance, openness, kindness? Where were relationships fostered, and when they failed, where did forgiveness and reconciliation occur? All the things that enabled you to grow as a human being can be included, because God is endlessly inviting you to life in its fullness.

And we mustn't leave out the natural world! We're part of the material universe and couldn't exist without it. God sets us in it and provides for us through it. Air, food, water, heat, light, and all the wonderful and beautiful things in creation play their part in God's gracing of us. Scripture tells us that God works in EVERYTHING for our good (Rom 8:28). This is a beautiful statement of what grace is about: God working in everything for our good.

Titles and Chapters

You'll have to think out chapter headings for your story. They'll become fully clear only as you go along. You may find it easiest to pick up your story in the present and work backwards. You may be tempted to classify your story as tragedy, but do so only provisionally, because the full story is not yet told. Its finest chapters have yet to be written, and we'll be sketching out their contours as we proceed. It's only in looking back that we can see the hand of God in our lives: like Jacob we find ourselves exclaiming, 'Truly God was in this place and I never knew it' (Gen 28:16). Like Peter we may protest about what is happening to us: then we need to learn patience and hear Jesus say to us, 'You do not know now what I am doing, but later you will understand' (Jn 13:7). Like Mary we are asked to store up our experiences, ponder them in our hearts (Lk 2: 19, 51), and learn from them that God is to be trusted because God is always on our side, not only when things are good but when they're at their worst. God is always working to bring good out of evil, however long it takes.

Escorts of Grace

If you begin with your birthday, try to recall who was there at the time, looking after you, loving you, forming a relationship with you. Certainly there was the family which received this new arrival, but also doctors, nurses and a wider supporting network of friends, neighbours and possibly the district nurse.

If you were well looked after, be aware that ultimately it was God who sent these 'escorts of grace' to you. They brought love and caring attention; they accepted you just as you were, and enabled you to get going in the journey of life. God desired to show you love when you were at your most fragile and dependent, and did so through the goodness of the people who were then around you.

If you were less fortunate, your early years may form one of the dark chapters of your story. God was still on your side, working steadily and undismayed even in the mess which others created for you. Perhaps your escorts of grace were unconventional, even unexpected? But notice how, consciously or unconsciously they tried to ease the bad situation and brought good out of pain, suffering and loss. The dark chapters take longer to write: they can be lonely and painful. Don't try to write them alone: ask God to show you who your substitute escorts of grace were when God's original choices failed in their tasks. Was there an aunt or uncle, a grandparent, a teacher or a good neighbour who helped in some way to lessen the damage done to you?

The Beloved of God

Early and later childhood will remind you of family life and school, youthful friendships, the discovery of the wonders of nature and of learning. Notice how God was present in all of these, but also how the Three Divine Persons introduced Themselves to you more personally, through prayers, Mass, devotions and symbols, and how your relationship with Them developed. Baptism was the first public initiative of

God in your regard. At that event the Three Divine Persons revealed their eternal choice of you as beloved daughter or son, and gave the Christian community the task of caring for you by good example and by nourishing you with the meaning of life and with food at the sacred meal which we call the Eucharist. I hope that the Christian Community gazed on you and smiled when you were baptized, just as God did!

We're back to smiles and meals and good relationships. The celebration of the Eucharist should mirror these rich realities.

Truly you are 'the beloved of God' (Rom 1:7). God cherishes you and labours to make a good place for you in our world. God is revealed to you as Care: your own uniqueness and giftedness come from God and reveal something of the uniqueness and giftedness of Godself.

In the next chapter we will sketch out further aspects of your autobiography, but once you catch on to the fact that God is in the ordinary and the everyday as the hidden dynamism which keeps your life going, then you will be able to recognise the truth of the final words of the curate in Bernanos' *Diary of a Country Priest*: '*All is grace. Grace is everywhere.*'

For Prayer

* Spend a little while sitting with Jesus or walking with him outside.

* Look back together at some event which brought a change in your life - begin with a happy event - and ask him to show you the grace hidden in it.

* You may feel you're a slow learner, but as you work along with Jesus the relationship between you is deepening all the time. Because you're searching, not on your own but with him, you become more sensitive to his delicate touch and recognise that he is truly and always out for your good.

For Pondering

What times of grace can you easily recognise in your life?

Chapter Three

Your Story Unfolds

This chapter opens out further ways of exploring the mystery and wonder of God's gracious involvement in your own life. Wherever you come upon situations where you've been helped, where people were there for you, you're touching on the working of grace in your life, because God is behind all people and situations which are helpful to you.

God is also present in bad situations, wrestling with them so that they may eventually work for our good. We will take up later this very important and difficult aspect of our relationship with God.

God on OUR Side

Only when we look back can we notice how God works for everyone's good. God wants no losers. It's easier to see this in good situations, but even in bad ones such as an unhappy marriage or the Northern Ireland troubles, we may stumble on the wonderful truth that God is on everyone's side, not simply on the side of the party who is 'right'. God makes the sun shine on the unjust as well as the just (Matt 5:45). Jesus is like his Father: he gets into endless trouble by being an indiscriminate host who welcomes sinners as well as the 'righteous.' Jesus does not exclude or take sides but tries to help everyone become truly human, alive and loving. Both victim and aggressor are God's concern.

A Good Start

In the last chapter you were invited to begin to notice some of the positive ways in which God has been present in the story of your life. Your birthday seemed the obvious place to start, and you were asked to recall who was there at the time, looking after you, loving you, and forming relationships with you. Through the goodness of these people God was trying to get you off to a good start in life. God works through people.

Beloved Child

We spoke of baptism as the way God reveals early on in a public way the divine choice of you as a beloved daughter or son. God places you within the Christian community so that you may become like Christ (cf Eph 4:13). It was as if God were saying to you: 'I've given you a human family but I also want to place you within my own family - the Christian family - which will provide you with good companions to help you on your journey towards the fullness of life.' To be included in the divine family is pure gift - grace!

20

Chosen Before the World Began

When you reflect further on your baptism in the light of Scripture, you'll notice that this choice of you goes a long way back: you were always the chosen one of God, chosen in Christ before the world was made (Eph 1:4). Imagine being chosen some 12 billion years ago! Imagine God holding steadily onto this choice as the universe developed, and the countless events that had to happen so that you could be born! That's a precious first chapter of our story but because it is written by God alone we can fail to advert to it. Contemporary scientists and theologians are now working together to make us aware of the fact that the story of the universe is our story, and that to tell the history of one person fully would require a history of the universe itself. Since all created reality is interdependent, our emergence into life is the fruit of incredibly intricate and careful planning on the part of God. You're a precious chapter of the world's history!

Pause and wonder about this for a little while, no matter how busy you may be. Twelve billion years deserve at least a five minute review! Then look around and contemplate the fact that 12 billion years have also been invested in everyone you meet today.

This can change your whole way of seeing people. That difficult person who breaks your heart is part of God's dream and cannot be discarded because God has invested hugely in him or her. God discards nobody. God always has been and will be for you both. Although perhaps you can do nothing practical to help others to change to a more gracious way of living, God invites you to be for them. By respecting them, praying for them and wishing them well you achieve more than you can imagine, as the following anonymous reflection indicates:

> What each one is interiorly face to face with GOD, unknown to anyone, is of vital consequence to all, and every act of love, every act of faith and adoration, every mute uplifting of the heart, raises the whole world nearer to God.

> From each one who is in union with God radiates a spiritual vitality, light, strength and joy, which reach from end to end of the universe, a source of grace even to those least worthy of it, even to those least conscious of it, and knowing nothing of how and whence it comes.

Carriers of Grace

Grace wants to be at work in every human interaction. We are meant to be carriers of grace for each other. We are in fact escorts of grace whenever we act lovingly towards those around us. In this sense grace operates both vertically and horizontally: grace comes to us 'from above' in the sense that God is always trying to get through to us directly in ways that will help us. God also tries to engage everyone who interacts with us to do so in ways that will be helpful. The whole web of human interconnections in your life is meant to be a sustaining web of grace. This is totally awesome.

Imagine how the present history of Northern Ireland would be transformed if this project of God were taken seriously. If only both sides could realise that God needs them to be carriers of good gifts to each other... If even one side could ask the question, 'How can we be helpful to the others?' it might be enough. When that becomes my question, my transformation gets under way, and so does the transformation of the world around me.

Mind and Heart of Jesus

'But being helpful to my enemy doesn't make sense; it's not rational!' somebody argued recently. 'That's true', someone else agreed: 'It doesn't make any human sense: it can't be worked out in your head, it's heart-stuff. Very often, loving doesn't make human sense, but maybe it makes a lot of divine sense, God-sense?'

God's attitude to us is steadily loving, unswervingly helpful, even when we're at our worst. Jesus tries to see what can best be done in bad situations. Even when he rebukes, he does so out of concern for the good of the other. He felt the pain of choosing to live this way: the pain was in his body, his mind and his heart. It broke him, broke him totally open, until there was nothing left for people to see, no reasonableness or intelligent planning, nothing but limitless love.

This was his final effort to show us just what God is like - limitless love, pure grace. We are invited to become like him. A favourite greeting card, sent to me years ago, reads, 'I simply love you'. That's what Jesus was trying to say to everyone, friend or enemy.

God Never Gives Up

The task of developing the attitude of Jesus is beyond any of us, left to ourselves. But it is not beyond God! God chooses to take on this task: it is God's primary activity in our world, and God works through all things and people to bring it about. This attitude of Jesus is developed in us: we 'become' this attitude! It's not something that we can achieve by our own efforts, but we can cooperate with its happening.

Put very simply, God not only works to be helpful to me at all times, but tries to get those around me to have the same helpful attitude towards me. Each person I meet is intended by God to be a carrier of grace to me; likewise, God needs me to be a carrier of grace to them.

'But why should I be nice to him? He's not nice to me!' This is where Jesus turns life upside down. He needs me to be helpful to that other person, in whatever way I can. This can sometimes mean tough love. The worse a person is, the more they need love rather than punishment. But to accept this would mean changing our whole penal system!

The Good News is that God never gives up, never stops trying to be helpful: perhaps our world is saved from falling apart by the fact that here, there and everywhere are found people who, whether they know it or not, are like God because they too never give up, they continuously want what is best for others. Speaking at his mother's funeral, a priest summed up her life as follows:

'The outstanding thing about my mother was that she was there, always, for all of us. Even in situations where she could do nothing to help us she was still there: she had space for us all and she prayed mightily for her children. She simply loved us; she accepted us just as we were; she helped us whenever she could and she asked God to help us. Often she seemed to be doing nothing and she sometimes wondered what her life was about, but it seems to me now that by having this loving and gracious attitude she had become exactly what God wanted her to be.'

From God's point of view, this very ordinary woman had achieved 'success' in life. She had taken on the attitudes of Jesus towards other people: we can sum up these attitudes as inclusion and compassion (cf Matt 5:43-48).

For Prayer

* Sitting with Jesus as you continue with your graced autobiography, try with his help to notice some of the people who were escorts of God's grace to you, people who were for you.

* How did they help to bring out the best in you, because that's what grace is about?

* Who showed you wise and sensitive love and helped you to believe that you are the beloved of God?

* Thank Jesus for whatever you discover.

For Pondering

'12 billion years in the making!' What does that open up for you about yourself, others and your world?

Chapter Four

The God Who Never Gives Up

Thus far the focus has been on the positive and more accessible aspects of your graced story. You've been invited to notice the people and situations which have helped you to grow and to become ever more fully alive. You have been looking at grace as God's constant working for our good in all things; God labouring for us with endless care. You have noted God's desire that everyone we meet would be an escort of grace for us, and that we in turn would be escorts of grace to them. You were invited to notice your escorts of grace and how they helped to bring out the best in you, because that's the goal of grace, the goal of God's love in action.

Dark Chapters

If you have persevered thus far, you will have come to a deep appreciation of grace in your life. But as hinted already, there are dark chapters in all our stories and they seem often to outnumber the happy ones. The Bible itself, though full of good news, has also been called 'The Book of Suffering' and the TV news often seems to be a round-up of the suffering of people across the world on a given day.

Human beings have the frightening capacity to be escorts of dis-grace rather than of grace to one another. Innocent people can find that those who could help them are in fact against them, depriving them of what they need for growth, life and joy.

Have we then the capacity to reduce God's dream to rubble? Does our inhumanity to one another paralyse the workings of grace? Do you feel that grace ran dry in certain situations of you life? Do you think that while others may have been more fortunate, for you it can't be true that 'All is Grace'? A tragic story from Maya Angelou's autobiography, *Gather Together in My Name* can help us here.

'I'm All he's Got'

She has just come back to her small home town, full of sophistication and city ways, and finding herself rejected by her friends she starts to drink heavily. Only one person stays with her, a lonely boy named L.C. Smith. Never popular because he was thought to be 'womanish', his mother had died when he was a baby, and his father drank moonshine even during the week.

'I was born here' he says, 'and will die here, and they've never liked me.' She asks him why he doesn't get away. 'And what would my Poppa do? I'm all he's got. Sometimes I bring home my salary and he drinks it up before I can buy food for the week. I've thought about going to New Orleans or Dallas, but all I know is how to pick cotton and hoe potatoes. Even if I could save the money to take Poppa with me, where would I get work in the city?

That's what happened to him, you know. After my mother died he wanted to leave the house, but where could he go? Sometimes when he's drunk he talks to her. 'Reenie, I can see you standing there. How come you didn't take me with you, Reenie? I ain't got no place to go, Reenie. I want to be with you, Reenie.' 'And', he concluded, 'I act like I don't even hear him.'

They shook hands and parted. The following year she heard that he had blown his brains out with a shotgun on the day of his father's funeral.

Even After Death

This story can serve as an example of the 'dead-end' suffering which is multiplied endlessly in human history. Evil dominates, grace is frustrated, God seems to be absent. Such stories in fact make many people despair of the existence of God at all.

How could a good God allow such dreadful things to happen to the people he is supposed to love?

Yet I believe that the Passion of Jesus can act as a torch to throw glimmers of light on such dark and distorted landscapes such as this story describes.

If we go back to our rule-of-thumb definition of grace as God Reveals And Calls Endlessly, then we can begin to sense that God's unwavering graciousness to us continues even after death. We can dare to believe that there are no limits to the distance which God will travel on our journeys; that God engages creatively in the consequences of our disastrous choices; that God's forgiveness is without boundaries and that the call to come home to light, joy and good company never goes silent.

We can believe that God goes into the realm of death and lostness and futility: the `descent into hell' affirmed in the Creeds is a symbol of grace still hard at work - Jesus sent by the Father to offer hope and friendship to those who in despair have settled for the weary destiny of endless alienation.

A Final Paragraph

With this background we can imagine a final paragraph to L.C.'s story, focussing on the father. It might go like this:

Soon after he died, L.C's father was shocked to find himself surrounded by a loving presence such as he had never known when he was alive. He seemed to be totally accepted: it was as if someone was gazing on him with immense and sensitive kindness; he was being smiled upon, and an intense level of communication had begun in which he was able to review his whole sorry life and find, to his amazement, that there was no hint of condemnation, only limitless understanding and compassion.

He was able to see what had driven him to act so harshly towards his son. Having had a hard upbringing himself, he had known no better than to treat his son the same way. His hardness and insensitivity began to melt away, and he cried tears of repentance which seemed to cleanse him to the depth of his being.

Overwhelming Desire

Through all of this he felt the strong and respectful support of the loving presence. One overwhelming desire erupted in his heart: to be able to meet his son and ask forgiveness. And suddenly L.C. stood before him: he sensed that they were both being embraced in infinite love and were being invited to embrace one another. They began to communicate with one another in ways never possible before. Each could tell his story, and the other accepted it.

It was as if they had begun to share in the very being of the loving presence who was showing both of them limitless understanding, reverence, compassion and acceptance. Welling up inside them was a limitless understanding, reverence, compassion and acceptance for each other. Their hearts were filled with gratitude, and the horrors of their years on earth faded like a bad dream.

Soon they found themselves in the presence of others whom they had known, everyone with their own story to tell, each a unique history of the triumph of grace....

So another rule of thumb definition of grace might be: God Reconciles And Consoles Everyone.

Summary

God never gives up. No matter how badly we distort our own lives and the lives of others, grace can still reach us, even after death. God is endlessly determined to bring us into good relationships with one another, not by force or magic, but by the gentle power of limitless love. God is the loving presence in which L.C. and his father and all other members of the family tree can meet and be reconciled.

For Prayer

* Decide on a time when you can meet to chat with Jesus. It's like making an appointment with a friend.

* Prepare the place: this time pull up three chairs rather than two. You invite Jesus in.

* In the security of the loving space which Jesus creates, you relax and feel accepted.

* Together you might agree to invite a third person to join you, someone who was a main figure in one of the dark chapters of your life.

* See what may happen when this person is invited into the loving space. You can be sure that Jesus will have time for both your stories......

For Pondering

Can you identify a 'dark' chapter in your life? Can you see that any good has come from it?

Chapter Five

Grace And Dis-Grace

Sometimes people and circumstances are against us. The following story illustrates the battle between grace and dis-grace through one person's lifetime. It can help us to see how God is For Us and works steadily through 'escorts' to remedy the damage which other people and circumstances can do to us.

As you reflect on your own story you'll certainly notice this theme. Adversity can wreak havoc in our lives but can also be an occasion for growth. When you see this for yourself you will have stumbled on the action of God who works away, often unnoticed, in the darkness, bringing good out of the most awful situations.

Conflicting Stories

'You're ugly as sin!' 'You're a useless article!' Her mother repeated these phrases over and over until the child believed them, deep, deep down. She knew she was a nuisance, and that she couldn't please her mother. But they struggled along together.

Many children who find that they are a burden to their parents develop problems which concretise their unacceptability: she developed serious and persistent weight problems. For her, being fat gave something to hide behind: being fat was safe. She worked very hard at believing she was ugly.

From her mid-life perspective she now sees that there were two conflicting stories about her as a child. One was the dark story, told by her mother, which as a child she tried hard to believe, because parents know! The reward for believing that story was that she would then be `in' with her mother, which she so desperately wanted, but the cost was enormous. The other was a kinder story, told by people in the family circle: there were those who liked her and made her feel good. This was confusing because it contradicted the 'true' story.

Self-Hatred

She was a disappointment to her mother, simply because she was a girl and not a boy. Beatings were frequent, but the constant putting-down was even worse. The daughter wanted more than anything that her mother would find her lovable. She hated being unlovable, and so she hated herself. She believed she was simply not to be loved. This led her to fear that she might contaminate others if they came too close.

Her father dreaded rows, so rather than standing up to his wife he tried to make up to his daughter by compensating her with money for sweets. The wife in fact needed her husband to stand up to her: when he failed to do so, the daughter got caught firmly in the middle.

No matter how often she tried classes in self-improvement and weight reduction, some other part of her held on to the habit of overeating, perhaps to show the world that her mother's comment, 'You're unacceptable!' was still true. Eating sweet things when unhappy compensated for the sour atmosphere around her.

An Escort of Grace

Things began to change when she met someone whose life was centred on a loving, gracious, big-hearted God. She had the choice of either just listening politely or of letting her heart be touched. She found herself bombarded with the good news that there are 'wonder-full' possibilities hidden in everyone and everything. Her unexpected friend became an escort of God's grace to her.

The flow of grace, by which she came to understand the kind regard of God for her, threatened to sweep her away, but the continuing 'evidence' of her own unworthiness stood in the way. 'I don't know how your husband puts up with you,' or 'You're a fool!' - such remarks from her mother almost capsized her little boat. But the longing to believe the Good News grew and grew, and the 'good story' began to make more and more headway against the bad one. The mould in which she'd cast herself began to fragment.

Ugly Feelings

When her marriage was threatened with breakdown, there emerged, with help from friends, a new movement towards truth and honest communication.

When she won a competition of skill, friends asked, 'Now, does that make you feel worthwhile?' But she felt it wasn't really she who had been successful: 'It was just learned knowledge,' she protested. There was still a long way to go from poor self-esteem to a proper appreciation of herself.

At a function one evening she met a woman who needed to be collected by her husband, but who found, to her amused dismay, that she had difficulty remembering her own phone number. Watching this trivial event, the daughter was shocked at finding in herself all sorts of ugly feelings towards this woman. Disdain, envy and jealousy were stirred up against someone who could ring her husband and know that he would be happy to come to collect her. 'She, who forgets her own phone number, is to be loved, and I, who would never be caught out like this, am not.'

Horrified at how judgemental she was, and how ugly her feelings were, she stumbled into an awareness that she had other ugly feelings, which before had been unthinkable and unspeakable.

From Truth to Freedom

She recalled that her mother, shortly before dying, had smiled at her with a 'pure' smile and that she had been unable to accept it. 'It's too late,' she said to herself, and closed her heart against her mother. For the first time in her life she acknowledged that she hated her mother. 'This,' she said afterwards, 'hit me as the worst thing anyone could say. I thought the world would collapse.'

Slowly she came to realize that love and hate can co-exist: as well as loving her mother, she also hated

36

her. Negative feelings, she learned, can be natural and healthy: like love itself, they can be used for good, or abused. Having dared to speak about this incident with a few trusted friends, she found they didn't turn away. She felt forgiven, and this was a key which enabled her to forgive both herself and her mother. The truth was setting her free, however painfully.

She noticed that her backache had flared up under the stress of speaking the truth. This led her to decide to do something about her health. 'I noticed a change of attitude in my heart towards myself: I'd become worth doing something for.' She had known for a while that the excess weight was linked with the backache. Now she found it relatively easy to avoid biscuits and other problem foods, and her health improved steadily.

Image of God

Previously her image of God was of an adult, impossible to please; someone who didn't like her but had to put up with her, because God was God! Just as she couldn't tell her father how she felt as a child because he was unable to carry it, she'd presumed that God couldn't carry the truth either and so prayer was largely a pretence. 'I was ashamed in front of my father because my mother found me so impossible. I felt I was a burden to him. If only I'd been different .....' And so she was ashamed in front of God too. How could God like someone whose mother didn't like her?

Such an image is gradually eroding. Jesus has become kind. He smiles easily. He likes her and is glad about her as truly as he was glad about his way-ward disciple Peter whom he liked as well as loved.

The Constancy of Grace

This story brings home to us the hope-filled realisa-tion that God doesn't simply create us and then leave us alone. Though we may feel that we are abandoned and left to flounder unsupported, the reality is other-wise. God works away steadily to make good the damage which others cause us. As in this woman's story, escorts show up in our lives to help us accept that we're truly lovable: this makes us happier about ourselves, about others, and about God. Grace, the 'good story', is winning through.

We could spend our lives grieving over the fact that the persons we want to love us don't do so. Then we're like the difficult child whose aunt brought him an armful of presents for his birthday, his mother having given him a fiver in an envelope. Having opened his gifts he still looked glum. 'What's wrong?' she asked, a bit rattled. 'I wanted the present you didn't bring!'

Certainly God wished the mother to be more lov-ing, But she wasn't, so God prompted the aunt to help the situation. Of course an aunt's love is not as good as mother-love, but we can get by with 'the next best thing' in an imperfect world where grace has to battle with dis-grace endlessly.

For Prayer

* Take some time to sit with Jesus.

* Think back over your life and notice any 'ugly' feelings towards someone you were 'supposed' to love, but didn't like!

* Try to chat with him about them.

* Notice that he doesn't turn away: instead watch him nodding and saying, 'I've known 'ugly' feelings myself: they helped me to come to the truth about people. I became freer and more able to accept them as they were - difficult yet beloved people for whom I was willing to die.'

For Pondering

Can you catch on to situations where expected escorts of grace failed to play their parts, but an unexpected escort did show up instead?

Chapter Six

Remedial Education In Loving

The fourth chapter centred on a boy who, having looked after his insensitive father until he died, committed suicide on the day of the funeral. We suggested how things might have unfolded for them when they found themselves together in God's presence. The point being made was that grace, which is God's creative activity in our lives, continues on even after death.

No Losers with God?

Likewise, the daughter whose story was related in the last chapter, has found that good things have gone on in her heart since her mother died. She has a sense now that with God there are no losers, that both she and her mother are of limitless importance to God. God knows and accepts the truth of both their stories.

> 'As for my mother, I hope she's basking in the warmth and kindness of God's loving smile, and that she's beginning to smile shyly back. No one in this world could

have healed her, and I'm happy that she now knows for the first time what it's like to be loved totally. I hope she'll come to see what really went on between us; I believe that she wouldn't want it to have been the way it was. I'd like her not only to love me, but to like me..... But I admit that there's a great deal about her which I could never like. I'm leaving it all in God's kind hands!'

Is this what really goes on after death? Is it only then, perhaps for the first time, that some people learn how well they are loved? When they are overwhelmed by this happy realisation, will they then be free to learn to love other people as God does, and even to like them?

Remedial Education

The joy of living can be dimmed by fear of how our story may end. We may also fear for others whose lives have been less than 'good'. When the full story of humankind is told, will we find many heartbreaking stories among the successes?

Firstly, a word about those whose love, when they die, is as yet limited and earth-bound. Death does not set time-limits to the Good News of God's welcoming love. The Catholic tradition of purgatory may well be understood as a process of remedial education in loving. Think of it, not as punishment, but as accelerated development! It is a final preparation for entry into the community of those who have learned to love without limits. Grace is all about relationships, and God calls us endlessly. Even after death God works to restore or develop to the full those relationships which were not good in this life. When L.C's father met God, the experience of coming face to face with limitless love for the first time was portrayed as a purging event, painful yet liberating and life-giving. L.C's father suddenly grows up and comes to love as adults should. Purgatory means conversion to one another. In this life we are meant to come to see the boundless demands of love, but if for whatever reason we kept our eyes shut, when we encounter God at the hour of our death our eyes will be opened.

Gracious People

Someone close to me died recently: life's trials, and they were many, had mellowed her, and by the time she became terminally ill she was known as 'that gracious lady'. I knew of only one relationship which was still blocked: she could not forgive her dead husband for their unhappy marriage. She died thus, and my prayer was that when she met God she would discover God's compassion both for her husband and herself, because she too had contributed to their unhappiness. The pain of purgatory is the pain of having to ask and to give forgiveness. Each partner would ask forgiveness of the other and thus they would become 'that gracious couple'.

What About Hell?

'So far so good', you may say, 'but what about those who die in mortal sin? Surely they are outside the 'catchment area' of God's remedial education? Is grace eternally frustrated in their case?' These questions must be taken seriously.

Because we are free, we are able to reject God, and while God's absolute and eternal love does not change or grow weak, neither can it force the loved sinner to love in return. God never by-passes human freedom in order to release us from the results of our free decisions nor does God ever condemn anyone to hell.

Rather, hell would be the decision to alienate oneself from God forever, a definitive rejection of Love itself, a radical turning away from a relationship which the sinner has known to be good and life-giving.

Whether anyone in fact has definitively rejected the real God, we do not know, nor has the Church ever dared to say that anyone has. In the Catholic Catechism (n.1861) we find the following cautionary and hopeful comment:

> *'ALTHOUGH WE CAN JUDGE THAT AN ACT IS IN ITSELF A GRAVE OFFENCE, WE MUST ENTRUST THE JUDGEMENT OF PERSONS TO THE JUSTICE AND MERCY OF GOD'.*

Some people die while seemingly in a bad relationship with others and so with God. We may feel that they are lost for ever, perhaps that they should be lost for ever! We feel, very humanly that they deserve their punishment. But we are told that we must entrust such persons to God. The Church's hope is that divine judging is wiser and kinder than ours.

The Real God

Definitive rejection of God would mean that a person irrevocably closes the door which leads to true life and joy, and the companionship of others. Does it happen?

When someone says, 'I reject God!' the 'God' in question often turns out to be a caricature of the God of Jesus Christ, and it is right to reject such false gods. The old catechisms began with the assertion that 'There is but one God, who will reward the good and punish the wicked.' Many feel that if this is the best one can say of God, they don't want anything to do with Him. Such a god is no better than an unimaginative earthly judge.

But who then is the real God? The real God means the three divine Persons who invest everything in Their project of bringing us all to the fullness of life. The real God has hope for us all, and is imaginative and infinitely resourceful. Father and Son are in full, loving agreement that one of Them should become totally involved in saving our world. It is as if the Son were saying, 'Please, can I go?' and the Father says 'Yes' and blesses him. The Son loves us to the uttermost (cf Jn 13:1), even beyond death. Through the resurrection he 'is with us always, until the end of time' (cf Matt 28:20).

The Spirit of Life puts new heart and spirit into us, and works steadily to complete the loving activity of Father and Son, thus bringing about 'the resurrection of the dead and the life of the world to come'.

Come To The Feast!

What God intends for humankind is the final community of love: in simple terms God is planning a
cosmic party. Everyone, without exception, is invited. It is the social event of the age, conceived in such
a way that everyone's happiness will be complete. To
grasp this as the project of the real God, and then
reject it, seems well-nigh impossible. It is your task
and mine, having caught on to God's dreams for us
all, to share this good news and to be the good news
in action to those who need it.

The real God is not mean or small-minded, nor
trying to catch people out. Sins of weakness and sudden lapses from goodness do not override the funda-
mental orientation of a good life. The statement that
'life is like a tight-rope with hellfire burning under-
neath - one slip and all is lost', is a travesty of the
truth about God. God always wants us: God never
changes on this. God simply is good and always
wishes the best for us. Divine love is steady, intense,
unmixed, unfazed by anything we get up to!

In the best of Christian thought, heaven and hell
are not equal possibilities. The chances of our getting
to heaven are far greater than our chances of ending
up in hell! Whereas the Church has never named
anyone as being in hell, the Communion of Saints is
an article of the Creed: heaven is densely populated!

Good News

Surprising as it may seem, Scripture, rightly understood, does not predict that at the End the world will
be divided into saved and lost. The parable of the

Last Judgement, for instance, is not a preview of the final situation: understand it instead as a dramatic warning about the importance of loving your neighbour: it is an urgent invitation to conversion, and in this sense, like the rest of the New Testament, it is 'Good News'. (cf Matt 25: 31-46).

Again let us look at the authoritative statements of the Catholic Catechism (nn. 1036, 1041):

> *'THE AFFIRMATIONS OF SACRED SCRIPTURE AND THE TEACHINGS OF THE CHURCH ON THE SUBJECT OF HELL ARE A CALL TO THE RESPONS-IBILITY INCUMBENT ON US TO MAKE USE OF OUR FREEDOM IN VIEW OF OUR ETERNAL DESTINY ... THEY ARE AN URGENT CALL TO CONVERSION ... THE MESSAGE OF THE LAST JUDGEMENT CALLS US TO CONVERSION WHILE THERE IS STILL TIME.'*

Notice how the Church, for all her faults, never-theless acts as a steady 'escort of hope' for all humankind. This is reflected in Vatican ll's sober optimism that on the Last Day 'humankind, saved by grace, will offer perfect glory to God as the family beloved of God and of Christ their brother' (cf 'The Church in the Modern World World' no. 32).

Hell Empty?

The hope that all will enjoy eternal life is based on the rock-solid ground, not of human goodness but of divine goodness. Hence we may join the line of

Christian witnesses - mainly female and in some cases canonised - who have clung to the belief that while hell is a possibility, it will never be inhabited. Julian of Norwich summed up her hope in the phrase, 'All will be well!' Another statement in the same tradition is, 'I believe in hell, empty!'

For Prayer

* When next you sit with Jesus and knowing it's safe to bring up any question,

* Ask him to explain again about the sort of love that's in God's heart for us when we're 'lost'.

* Hear him tell you about God searching until he finds, as in the story about the lost sheep or the lost coin (Lk 15:4-10).

* Hear him say, 'I care this much about you and everybody else too, and I'd love you to believe this and to care for others in the same way'.

For Pondering

Think of a person significant to you, now dead, with whom you got along poorly. How do you picture this person now in relation to you?

Chapter Seven

Dare We Hope?

'I believe in hell, empty!' This statement, rooted in the New Testament itself, sums up the inexhaustible hope of a long line of Christian thinkers, that all of us may eventually be saved. In the context of this hope, we continue here to explore the role of grace, even after death.

'But what place,' you may ask, 'has this theme in my life story?' The reality is that all our stories are inextricably linked together, so that what happens to even one person affects all the others. If one person, one member of my extended family, were to be lost, would I mind? Would others mind if I were to be lost? Our relationship with God is not a private affair! It must include concern for the others, all the others, because they are in solidarity with me and I with them. I can't disown them. If the place reserved for me at the great feast were empty, that would affect everybody else and if even one other place were empty that would affect me. Religion is not a private but a social affair. God is social, so we must be also. God watches out for everyone and so must we, however demanding it may be.

'I Love You Still'

Hitler's holocaust of the Jewish people was the most dis-graceful event of the twentieth century. Let us dare to picture the scene when Hitler and God met face to face. God, knowing all that has gone on, still meets him gently and brings him to a totally honest awareness of how his life has been. They look together as God's light illuminates all his darkness. Might Hitler cry out, 'You can't possibly want to have anything to do with me now. Eliminate me!' But God says, 'I love you still! I'm inviting you in; there are others here who wish you well and want to meet you. But you will want to ask forgiveness of everyone whom you hurt. They will forgive you: have no fear about that!'

And so they go in together and he finds himself, to his amazement, met with respect and kindness. People whom he had destroyed now sit with him: they explore together the truth of things. Appalled by their stories, Hitler might well fall apart but is somehow held by love. He and his victims come by God's grace to reconciliation. Then there is joy in heaven, joy for everyone because Hitler is included (cf Lk 15:7).

A Small Grain of Love

A favourite theologian of Pope John Paul ll, von Balthasar, suggests that in judging us, God will search to see if anywhere at all in the sinner there is something, even a small grain of love, which could be receptive to divine love. Surely, we can dare to hope that even the worst of us is loved by someone and so is held from sinking into nothingness?

Thomas Merton in *Conjectures of a Guilty Bystander* asserts that in all of us, without exception, there is a point 'which is untouched by sin, a point of pure truth, a point or spark which belongs entirely to God, and which is never at our disposal. It is the pure glory of God in us and is inaccessible to the fantasies of our minds or the brutalities of our wills' (p. 158).

It is as if there's a little bit of God which we bring with us, as a child carries something of its parents: it is the almost invisible golden thread of grace: it is there because God wants it there. The first effect of grace is to make each and all of us 'the beloveds of God'. Wayward we may become, but always we remain beloved. Are we all, then, wayward beloveds?

The fact is that God doesn't want to lose us ever, and so holds on to us no matter how far we might stray. There is then a grain of eternal love in everyone, which gives real hope that all of us will reach eternal life. In G. M. Hopkins' phrase, we are 'immortal diamonds' and diamonds are forever!

On the Way Back

Four-year-old David announced that he was leaving home. He had been talked out of this drastic step several times before, but this time he was really going! His mother helped him to pack his rucksack: a clean pair of underpants, his toy dog 'Wow-wow' and some Ladybird books. Off he went in his bright orange raincoat, she following at a safe distance. When he reached a main road which he had never crossed alone he turned back, and she discreetly appeared at the half-way stage and escorted him home.

This little tale tells us something about God, who respects our freedom and lets us go our chosen ways, but is still totally engaged in watching out for our good. God's love is mirrored in that mother's love, but while her resources were very limited, God's are without bounds. God's drawing of us, we may rightly believe, will be irresistible in the long run. Sinners, exhausted by their weary journey away from God, may stop to rest only to find the welcoming gleam of 'home' right beside them.

Judges and Examiners

Can we accept that God's 'judging' is much more like the 'judging' of that loving and anxious mother than the judging of human judges and examiners? Defendants in law courts hope for a sympathetic judge, but judges have to give verdict in accordance with the evidence. Likewise, no matter how examiners may feel about you, if you get the right answers, you pass: if not, you fail. An examiner could take a dislike to you or be biased in your favour, but in a written exam this will make no difference. The result depends on you, not on the examiner.

Such models as judge and examiner do little justice to God, who is not neutral and dispassionate, but is instead totally and passionately on our side, and on everyone's side. God indeed 'judges' but always in our favour. We must allow our thinking and our hearts to be turned upside down and inside out if we're to catch on to the 'outrageous' prodigality of God.

Good News for the Bad

Imagine the following courtroom scene in which the jury has brought in a 'guilty' verdict against a set of criminals.

The judge then speaks: 'I accept the verdict, and I've also decided to forgive and acquit them: they may go free!'

The prosecutor jumps to his feet: 'What about the damage they've caused?'

'I will pay the costs and make good all damages' responds the judge quietly.

'But you can't do that: that is a travesty of law and order.'

'Ah yes, I can do this, and I will do it. I would treat you all in the same way if you were brought before me, so none of you can feel cheated of justice. Can't you be glad that I'm merciful? Have you no feeling for the criminals? They are human beings like yourselves ...'

Such a verdict would get world attention. In explaining to the media his extraordinary stance, the judge might tell the story of a man who had two sons, the younger of whom said, 'Father, let me have the share of the estate that would come to me ...' It would be the story of the prodigal Father who reinstates his wayward beloved son to the amazement of all and the resentment of some (Lk 15: 11-32).

Bad News for the Good?

Do you find yourself reacting strongly to the last paragraph? When Jesus told the story of the prodigal father, many of his listeners must have found themselves lining up in sympathy with the elder brother.

There are many 'righteous' people who trust in their own good performance, who would stand up to God at judgement time and demand entrance into heaven.

Could it be that the 'righteous' people rather than the sinners will be the main problem in the path of God's project of bringing everyone to heaven? The Gospels infer as much: 'The tax collectors and sinners were all seeking the company of Jesus, and the Pharisees and the scribes complained' (Lk 15:1-2).

In as much as there's a streak of the elder brother in us, we don't yet know the real God. We wouldn't feel very much at home in heaven, because we'd be angry with the sinners we'd find there, and with the God who was letting them in.

Our hearts must be broken open until our hospitality and compassion match those of God. Grace will finally triumph only when the 'No!' of the `righteous' is changed to a resounding 'Yes!' of acceptance of all the others whom God has decided to invite to the Wedding Feast. None will be there by right or by merit. Grace is gift, so all will be there by God's free invitation.

What began as your story and seemed fairly manageable is turning out to involve everyone else's story too, and is leading to a new view of God as more and more mysterious and incomprehensible and wonderful. You might find that you include in your story a very rich chapter titled simply, 'GOD'.

For Prayer

* When you sit with Jesus again perhaps you might enter into the following dialogue:

* 'Lord, tell me about this 'Yes' of yours towards the 'good' and the 'bad', because I don't think that way. I divide the good from the 'others'.

* He replies, with a twinkle in his eye: 'And which group do you put yourself into?'

* You're silent for a while, perhaps because you're stuck?

* He goes on: 'For me there aren't two groups. I simply love you all exactly as you are and I'd like you to love everyone else in the same way. It hurts me when people say to God, 'You shouldn't let those people in'. This is to miss the whole point about grace - it's a free gift to you all, and isn't merited by people's goodness'.

For Pondering

How do you feel about the possibility that everyone may be saved? - Including yourself?

Chapter Eight

Happy Ending

A story needs an ending. Will the human story end in catastrophe or triumph? Let us continue here to look ahead to catch some glimpse of the possible outcome of your story and mine and that of everybody else.

We have noted that God rather than ourselves has the central role at the last judgement. The final event of human history will not simply be a rubber-stamping or a freezing into eternity of what we've done in time. It will not be a simple acknowledgement of the sad state of human affairs, not a neutral and dispassionate taking-stock, nor a boring summing up of what we know already. It would not take a God to tell us that things are bad: we could do that ourselves!

Master of Ceremonies

What then will Judgement Day be like? God is the hidden Master of Ceremonies, the unimaginably creative being who brings order out of chaos in the act of creation, brings good out of evil in the passion of Jesus and life out of death in the resurrection. Against all expectation the pattern of divine interventions is to bring life out of death and hopelessness. The last judgement in turn will be the high point of God's boundless creativity.

Every action of God is life-giving: this must be so because God simply is life and cannot but share life with us. God's desire is for us all to have the fullness of life, and we can dare to hope that God will finally achieve this desire.

We can rightly hope that judgement is the final proclamation of the Good News for ourselves and everyone else, the ultimate expression of the passionate and extravagant love of God for humankind. Judgement can be viewed as creative, life-giving, surprising, the final triumph of grace. Just as the first proclamation of grace gave rise to amazement and joy among the tiny band of followers of Jesus 2,000 years ago, we may hope that its final proclamation will lead to endless amazement, joy and gratitude when we find that the Good News includes us all.

All Will Be Well

In the year 1373 the English hermit Julian of Norwich was puzzling over the fate of those who die in mortal sin. Speaking with her Lord in prayer, it was revealed to her that 'there is a deed which the blessed Trinity will perform on the last day. Just as the blessed Trinity made all things from nothing, so they shall make everything well which is not well.'

This was beyond her understanding, so our Lord continued: 'What is impossible to you is not impossible to me: I shall make everything well and you will see yourself that every kind of thing will be well.'

What the 'deed' may be, by which 'all will be made well' is an unfathomable mystery: Julian's conviction is rooted in a right sense of the greatness of

God, which alone can justify the hope of the salvation of all and the total triumph of grace.

Her conviction echoes that of St Paul: 'Glory be to God whose power working in us can do infinitely more than we can ask or imagine' (Eph 3:20). And again: 'God's purpose is to show mercy to all humankind. How rich are the depths of God - how deep God's wisdom and knowledge - and how impossible to penetrate God's motives or understand God's methods' (Rm 11: 32-33).

In fairy-tales a sudden twist just before the end turns tragedy into joy and brings about 'happy endings'. We can dare to hope that the unexpected intervention of 'the Prince' in the tragic tale of human history will transform sorrow into endless joy.

Upside-down

Our neat and all too human images of judgement simply won't do when we try to grapple with God's judgements. They are too small, too earth-bound; they are unworthy of God. 'My thoughts are not your thoughts, my ways not your ways. The heavens are as high above earth as my ways are above your ways, as my thoughts are above your thoughts' (Isaiah 55:8-9).

This statement is radical good news: It needs to be taken with total seriousness as an invitation to let go of our narrow and fear-filled ways of judging. If we apply it to the issue of Judgement after death we will find that it brings a sense of hope for ourselves and for everyone else and gives us a new appreciation of God as infinitely loving and welcoming.

Passed Already

Scripture makes clear that God will judge the world, and also that God has already passed judgement on the world and that that judgement is favourable. God has already ruled in favour of the human race: the heart of St John's Gospel is the statement, God loved the world so much as to give God's only son (3:16).

St Paul comments rapturously on this theme: 'With God on our side who can be against us? Could anyone accuse those that God has chosen? When God acquits, could anyone condemn?' (Rm 8:31-34). Divine judgement then, has already been made in our favour: God does acquit, and for this let us all be grateful!

But is our acquittal simply the wiping clean of the slate of our lives, as if the evil we'd done didn't matter? It can't be so: the evil does matter, but God's grace is so wonderful that it brings good out of evil. Grace is always present even in the darkest times and mysteriously manages to use the very darkness in order to bring light. A discordant note becomes the first note of a new theme in the divine symphony.

'Forgive my Enemies'

A Jewish person wrote the following prayer on a piece of wrapping paper before entering the gas chamber. This message from the Holocaust illustrates dramatically how evil people can bring about good in spite of themselves and become unexpected escorts of grace to those whom they hurt.

'Lord, when you enter your glory, do not remember people of good will only.
Remember also those of ill will.
Do not remember their cruelty and their violence.
Instead, be mindful of the fruits we bore because of what they did to us.
Remember the patience of some and the courage of others.
Recall the camaraderie, humility, fidelity, and greatness of soul which they awoke in us.
And grant, O Lord, that the fruits we bore may one day be their redemption.'

Such greatness of heart is rare, but if a single human heart can forgive in this way, the divine heart must be infinitely more forgiving. The extent of the wrong done makes the forgiveness all the more magnificent. God is magnificent, as the parable of the prodigal father illustrates. In thinking of final judgement let us keep an eye on that prayer always.

Lastly: Forgive others and you are guaranteed that God will forgive you. 'If you forgive others their failings, God will forgive you yours' (Matt 6:15). What an extraordinary promise! It is not the sinner but the unforgiving who risk exclusion. Only the unforgiving heart is out of place in the kingdom of God.

Outwitting Evil

The extraordinary prayer above echoes in concrete form the thought of Edith Stein. She points out that grace can and does enter the human heart unsought, and can steal into the heart of the sinner, winning ground and repelling the effects of sin. To this process of displacement, there are, in principle, no limits. Human freedom cannot be broken by divine freedom, but it may well be, so to speak, outwitted. The gift of grace is a free act of divine love, and there are NO LIMITS to how far it may extend.

The social implications of all of this are huge. If we think that God simply 'punishes the wicked' then we feel justified in doing likewise. But if we come to believe that God calls endlessly to the wicked, then we must do the same. How we view final judgement determines our present attitudes. If we believe that God tries right to the End to be inclusive of everyone, then we must work for the rehabilitation of criminals so far as possible.

Now we can de-code GRACE as: God Rescues And Claims Everyone!

For Prayer

* You might sit with Jesus who listens attentively to you as you read again the Jew's prayer. He sees that such forgiveness is difficult for you.

* You turn to him and ask him about it: ask him to explain it.

* He invites you to look at his passion. He endured so much from evil people, but out of the pain patiently borne, something wonderful became visible to the world - the unimaginable love of God for humankind at its worst.

* Together you look back now at your own 'passion'. Can you see even the smallest glimmer of light? Did some tiny good come out of the breaking of your heart?

For Pondering

If you feel you've spoiled another's life in some way, can you believe that God makes good the damage?

Chapter Nine

The Law Of The Cross

The suggested exercise of the previous chapter invited us to look at how good can be drawn out of the darker aspects of our lives. How does this happen? How does God 'manage' the existence of evil? How does grace wrestle to transform the widespread disgrace that disfigures our world? This is a central issue in our life stories.

Grace Prevailed

The Railway Man is the extraordinary story of Eric Lomax, a Scotsman fascinated by trains, who became a prisoner of war after the fall of Singapore in 1942. Following three dreadful years of imprisonment and savage torture for possessing a radio, he was released in 1945 and tried to settle back into civilian life. But the inner wounds he had endured remained open for almost the next 50 years.

Hatred for his torturers consumed him: he yearned to know whether they had been brought to justice. He finally met one of his tormentors who had by then repented, and went through a world of inner struggle before he could speak his forgiveness to him. The final words of the book are: 'Sometime, the hating has to stop.'

It took 50 years to displace the hatred in Lomax's heart, but finally grace prevailed and good came out of the evil. For 50 years God was busily working away on both hearts: God gently brought the Japanese to an awareness of the evil he and his country had done, and brought Lomax through the dark valley of hatred to the moment of forgiveness. Lomax came to see his former torturer as a human being with a broken and open heart.

Has Suffering Any Meaning?

As Christians, what attitude are we asked to take up in the face of the unavoidable suffering which comes our way? So much of life seems just to 'happen to us': we don't choose ill health or destitution or a failed marriage or a severely handicapped child. We don't choose to get mugged, or be hit by a drunken driver or to be tortured.

We can do nothing but endure the deaths of those we love, and finally our own deaths. So much is outside our control. Often people say: 'Things didn't work out; they fell apart despite my best efforts.'

We endure a great deal, but is it a matter of simply enduring? Can grace perhaps penetrate even into the worst of human situations, from which there is no escape, and bring life and meaning to them? How would you respond to the following:

'My mother suffered from arthritis most of her life: towards the end she was bent double, and five months before she died, her back literally broke. What she endured after that I can only call crucifixion, and when sitting with her in her pain the thought used cross my mind that although Jesus suffered terribly on the cross, he died very quickly, while my mother's agony went on and on and on.'

Is there any value, any meaning in such pain?

The Law of the Cross

There is a profound belief in Christian spirituality about suffering, which has been called The Law of the Cross. Its simplest statement is:
UNAVOIDABLE SUFFERING, PATIENTLY ENDURED, IS GRACED.
The humble Morning Offering enshrines it: 'I offer the prayers, works and sufferings of this day for all the intentions of your Sacred Heart.'

Let us look at this Law of the Cross in some detail.

Unavoidable Suffering

Firstly, note the word 'unavoidable'. Physical or emotional suffering which can be avoided or cured, must be fought against: like Jesus we are to engage in the struggle against injustice and oppression. Whatever is demeaning to human dignity, whether in the wider world or in the home, should arouse a protest in us. Personal dignity is a primary Christian value: each of us is the beloved of God, and we must never betray this truth.

Feminists say that if pride is men's original sin, for women original sin is passivity. A great sign of hope in our times is the gradual movement among women away from passivity. 'Peace at any price' is no longer seen as a healthy or graced attitude.

Nevertheless some suffering simply is unavoidable.

Patiently Endured

When faced with unavoidable suffering we can find ourselves feeling angry, bitter and resentful. We may decide to endure it with stoic resignation, or we may feel we deserve it, that God is punishing us for our wrongdoing. The twist on that is expressed in the phrase: 'God must love you very much to send you so much pain!' Such spiritualising in order to find meaning in pain is totally unworthy of God and ourselves.

The basic example of patient enduring is that of Jesus in the passion. Notice how much space in the gospels is taken up with his passion and death. These dark chapters of his life have become the key chapters in his whole story. They teach us a vital lesson about suffering and show us how grace can win out in the face of pain and evil.

Example of Jesus

Jesus had a choice: he could have died screaming resentment against his persecutors and his God for being so atrociously mistreated. Instead he chose to bear with patient love what had to be endured. He did not believe that his Father was responsible for the suffering, but he did trust his Father to see him through it. His Father did not fail him but brought him through suffering and death into the fullness of divine life. The Father endorsed his attitude of patient and loving endurance, because in this way he revealed new dimensions of God's love never guessed before.

The attitude of Jesus in the Passion is like a 'headline' which we must keep our eye on and learn to copy. This is the key which transforms the dark chapters of his life and of ours if we choose. During our dark times we are as totally loved by God as in our joyous times, so the darkness is not totally black: it is already graced. What is supremely important is for this gracious love which penetrates our darkness to find the answering gleam of our patient acceptance of what we have to endure. But let's not be too surprised at ourselves to find this attitude co-existing with bouts of raging anger and resentment, for we're only human.

Graced Suffering

What do we mean by saying that unavoidable suffering, patiently endured, is graced? Throughout these pages we have been stressing the fact that God is busily working in every situation of our lives, trying to help us to grow to the fullness of what we can become. This is what we mean by grace.

Jesus chose to continue loving right through the passion and thus revealed to us the limitless depths of his love. The suffering became a means of revealing that love: had Jesus taken the opposite attitude the suffering would have led to hatred, alienation and despair.

The choice was his, just as it is ours whenever we are forced to suffer. It helps greatly to know that grace is always working with us in our suffering to strengthen us and to save us from being overwhelmed by it.

Grace in our Dying

In his sensitive book, *Mortally Wounded*, Michael Kearney shows that as long as terminally ill cancer patients resist the truth of their dying, their physical and psychological discomfort can be acute. But in those who come to the attitude proposed in the 'Law of the Cross' something mysteriously eases, and their medication can be reduced, often dramatically.

Kearney comments: 'In our dying, and in our working with those approaching death, there is another world and another work that wishes us and all our efforts well.'

It is in fact God's eternal world which is opening up; it is grace which is at work, enabling us to grow in love by patiently accepting this final letting go. Does this help you as you look ahead to the final chapter of your life?

For Prayer

* Sitting quietly with Jesus, you might hold a crucifix and just look. After a while of chatting with him about his suffering and death and how he faced them you might bring up something which you're going through at the moment or the prospect of your own death.

* Ask him for the grace to be able to trust the Law of the Cross in this situation, just as he did in his dark times.

* Hear him say, 'No matter what you're going through now, or will go through, try to be patient and loving. You're not alone. I'm very close to you.'

For Pondering

Identify some instances of unavoidable suffering in your life. Can you see how they link in with the passion? Has some good come from them?

Chapter Ten

Becoming Like God

A friend and I were chatting about grace. She said, 'I like the notion that my story and everyone else's is a graced story. But I wonder where does grace stop? What's God's ultimate dream for us?'

These are profound questions. Does grace do more than enable us to live our lives better? Does it reach into the very fibres of our being and bring about our transformation, so that, incredible though it may seem, we BECOME LIKE GOD?

Windows on our future

The Gospels make extravagant promises about our future which can fascinate and excite us; they point to change or transformation in us. For instance, those who accept Jesus are given power 'to become daughters and sons of God' (Jn 1:12). What must it be like to be a daughter or son of God? How will the family likeness show itself in us? 'Just like his father!' we sometimes say of a child. But what's the Father like?

Again, Jesus says: 'I have come so that they may have life ... to the full' (Jn 10:10): what can it mean 'to be full of the life of God'? How different that would make us, because we often feel `half-dead'!

Also, we are told that we shall become like God, because we shall see God as God is (1 Jn 3:2). This promise is referred to in funeral Masses to give us hope about those who have died. To see God will transform us: what will we then be like?

Lastly, we are promised that we 'will be able to share the divine nature' (2 Pt 1:4). Will we truly have the same nature as God? What stretching is needed in us to `accommodate' God?

What are all these promises hinting at and how will they come about?

Changes

Notice how many things change when Jesus comes: water becomes wine; bread and fish are multiplied; sick people are healed; the dead are raised; bread and wine are transformed into the person of Jesus. Jesus's own body is transfigured on the mountain.

People change through encountering him. They grow and see new and undreamed of possibilities in themselves: recall the woman at the well, Peter and Matthew, and so many others who accepted him. Life takes on new dimensions of meaning for them all in his company. This doesn't necessarily mean that life gets any easier for them: those around them may resent the change.

Jesus dreams dreams for people: he accepts them completely as they are and also sees their potential: he knows what the human person can become. As people catch on to his dreams for them they are enabled to move towards 'the fullness of life'.

Fullness of Life

What is this 'fullness of life'? It is linked with what
Jesus himself is, for he IS the 'fullness of life' - he is
fully human and also fully divine. He invites people
to enter into an unrestricted relationship with himself
and become as he is.

He has a totally open relationship with others, and
with 'Abba' his Father. We're invited to share in
these relationships. This happens as we fulfil the
command to open our hearts towards all our brothers
and sisters - 'Love one another!' He tells us too to
pray to be totally open to 'Abba' our Father - 'Your
will be done: Your Kingdom come.'

Could it be that the 'fullness of life' is to be found
centrally in good relationships, both human and
divine? Could it be that as we grow in openness to
others and to God, we are moving towards the fullness of life?

We may be quite unaware of this: many people
have no explicit belief in God, and yet they try to live
in right relationships with others and accept reality as
it comes to them. Thus, whether noticed or not, grace
is at work in their lives: grace often travels incogni-
to! But our story has so much more colour if we
know what is going on!

Human and Divine Dimensions

Perhaps we grow in two dimensions at the same
pace: as we become more fully human - more truly
loving - we are by that very fact becoming more fully
divine, because God is the fullness of what it means
to be truly loving.

Even in this life, then, we are being initiated into the life of God, which is love. Those who enter into relationship with Jesus and who love one another already possess eternal life. We don't have to wait! The eternal is not a future event - it is already present all around us. God is constantly working in our sin-damaged environment and that work will be completed when the atmosphere in which we live is fully loving.

We live in a divine milieu. When it succeeds in irradiating us through and through the reign of God will be complete in us. This is God's work.

What is really going on then beneath the surface of things is our divinising. Already fully realised in Jesus, it is the free gift, the grace, the marvellous mystery behind all the mysteries of life. It is offered to us all without exception and gives hope to every-one. More than that, it is already in process here and now, and we rightly hope it will be achieved in everyone. Grace, God's-love-in-action, is tough and durable and achieves its goal.

Drawn Into Life

The life of the world to come is already around us, affecting us deep down. What God is doing is draw-ing us ever further into that life. 'Drawing' is an important word in John's Gospel. It is the primary activity of God: God draws everyone into divine relationships. 'No one can come to me unless the Father draw them' (Jn 6:44): by this Jesus means, not that some are selected and others not, but that it is the Father who is drawing everyone to Jesus who is the fullness of life.

On the eve of his Passion, Jesus makes it clear that the scope of the drawing is universal: 'When I am lifted up from the earth I shall draw ALL people to myself' (Jn 12:32). Recall the code in the word GRACE: God Reveals And Calls Endlessly. Wherever God sees someone, God calls out to them.

Bringing Out the Best

Grace is all about good relationships. Relationships develop through people knowing and loving one another and sharing life together. Through our relationships we are transformed.

When one person in the relationship is divine, as Jesus is, then he transforms us by sharing with us his life and love and his own relationship with his Father. This brings out the best in us: we discover that we have a capacity for limitless life and love, but we need Jesus to awaken and fulfil this potential: we can't do it of ourselves.

This is GRACE, the totally unexpected and free gift of God's own life to us. Let us not limit the free gift by imagining that God wouldn't want to gift us in this way: it is a free gift, in no way depending on our merits. The Three Divine Persons simply decide to give Themselves to us: this cannot but change us radically so that we become like Them. On the human level we become like our friends: we develop similar ways of thinking and feeling about important issues: we live out of the same values. The same process occurs when one of our friends is Divine. We come to share Jesus' values, mindset, heart.

Surprised By Joy

There are no ordinary mortals around us: all of us are extraordinary immortals, to be reverenced limitlessly because each is destined for eternal glory. To decode our umbrella word GRACE in a new way: at the End grace will become Glory Revealed As Communal Ecstasy. This catches the sense that we will all be glorious together, in the happiest event of all time.

Let us then be surprised by joy at what God is doing, and allow God's dream to dominate our imaginations and hearts as we go about our lives. The new perspectives which open up in this chapter invite us to see our story in a new way. We catch on to what our Co-Author has in mind.

We began with two questions: 'Where does grace stop? What is God's dream for us?' I hope that they have now been answered to some extent. They give rise however to a further question: 'But how will it all happen?' This will be the theme of the next chapter.

For Prayer

* This time, as you sit or walk along with Jesus, you dare to ask him a serious question: 'What are you really up to?'

* 'I invite people to become my friends. I love doing that because to me everyone is wonderful in a deep down way. I see what they can become - there are no limits. There're all sons and daughters of my Father, you see; nobody is finished growing. For me, life is about helping people to grow in the wonder and appreciation of themselves and one another.'

* Perhaps you can hear him say to you, with a smile: 'If you're happy about it, you and I can go a long way together - all the way to the 'fullness of life'!'

For Pondering

'What is essential is invisible to the eye.' Are you catching on to the fact that over the years in a hidden way your heart is being softened, widened? Are you easier to live with?

Chapter Eleven

Loving Without Limits

We ended the last chapter with the question: 'How do we become like God? How will it all happen?' We will now explore the furthest reaches of the world of grace, in order to grasp in some limited way what God has in mind for us and how God goes about the work of sanctifying us all and bringing us to the fullness of life.

Live through love

Our entry into this world comes about because we are chosen by God. 'Even before the world was made, God chose us, chose us in Christ, to be holy and spotless, and to live through love in God's presence, becoming adopted sons and daughters ... to make us praise the glory of God's grace, the free gift to us in the Beloved.' (Eph 1:4-6).

We are chosen, then, to live through love in God's presence, and this is the vital clue as to how God divinises us, or makes us become like God. The clue is: 'Live through love.' We are made to live in the love of others, and in turn to live lovingly in relation to others and to God. Insofar as this is going on, we are becoming like God who is love itself.

God Takes the Initiative

The work of our divinisation is essentially God's, who takes all the great initiatives. Prior to our awareness or consent, we are oriented towards what the New Testament calls the Koinonia - the mysterious and wonderful network of relationships which include the three divine Persons, our neighbour and ourselves. This is a friendship of a new kind which is begun by Jesus.

A happy family provides a wonderful setting for a child to receive love and to learn how to love. Baptism makes us visible members of the Christian community in which we are meant to find ourselves loved, cherished and enabled to grow to the fullness of love.

The process continues in us even if the meaning of our lives eludes us, as it seems to elude so many people, but God invites us to catch on to what is happening and to go with it. The intended theme of our lives is, in the words of the second Eucharistic prayer, that we should 'grow in love'. When we do, we begin to say 'Yes' more and more, and begin to recognise the strong and delicate hands of God shaping our destiny in all the events which go to make up our personal story.

Who am I?

As we catch on we begin to develop in a serious way the relationships that constitute the companionship of the Koinonia. The interior life begins to flourish: its foundation is the humbled awareness that I am the beloved of God; the three divine Persons desire and work for the very best for me; They want to give Themselves to me. This is how it is also between Them and every other person on the planet: each of them is also the beloved of God, and so all my relationships are to be conducted in the light of this awareness.

Who am I? I am the beloved of God, no matter how wayward, and I am to be loved by all others. Who am I? I am to love God 'with all my heart and strength and mind' (Matt 22: 37), and I am to love my neighbours, all of them, with the same love as Jesus shows to me: 'Love one another as I have loved you' (Jn 15:12).

Loved and Loving

I am infinitely loved: as the Father loves Jesus - limitlessly - so does he love me (Jn 15:9). I am greatly loved and lovable; and in turn great love is asked of me. The love which flows to me in unrestricted fashion must flow unrestrictedly out towards others. To horde it up in myself puts my neighbour at risk of starving for lack of that love which alone gives true life.

I am asked to be creative in my loving; not to wait until I am sure it will find an echo in another. I am to risk my love into the emptiness, the warpedness perhaps, of the love-starved heart of another. This will generate situations in which I am totally vulnerable and exposed: I may sometimes have no other protection than the love with which God loves me but from which nothing can separate me: 'NOTHING can ever come between us and the love of God made visible in

Christ Jesus our Lord' (Rom 8:39). Will there be enough love to go around? The answer partly depends on me.

No Barriers to Love

The stretching of my heart goes on endlessly and often comes to breaking point. The demands of relationships of the most intimate and the most ordinary kind bring this about: marriage, parenting, friendships, and all the tangle of people living together and trying, by fair means or foul, to hold their place in the world.

God works in all these events, whether they be good or bad, joyous or painful, until I become a person without barriers, limits, boundaries. I become instead an accepting and inclusive person. I exclude nobody from my heart. I find myself praying not only for all those I love, but for those whom I would in an earlier phase have called my 'enemies'. I wish well to everyone.

More and more I come to accept God, and to accept in faith that God is working in all the events that touch my life, whether they be happy or painful. My weaknesses and my diminishments gain a new meaning: through them I am becoming 'space for love'.

Even my death begins to take on that meaning; it is the moment when I shall be totally empty space for God. I look beyond death in trembling hope to the mystery of my resurrection, my rising to the fullness of life and of love, for which all my life will then be seen to have been an infinitely wise and rich preparation.

A Place is Waiting

In St. Exupery's famous story the fox remarked to the Little Prince, 'The essential is invisible to the eye.' We need to catch on to the 'essential' and to make it known to others. The secret is that we are brothers and sisters of Jesus and that his divine inheritance has become ours: a place is waiting for us all in the world of the resurrection.

The Father wants to delight in us, rejoice in us, dance with us, and share with us the gift of his own boundless creativity and life. In God's company we shall find ourselves loved and appreciated in a manner that will be totally transforming and satisfying. We shall be totally 'Joy' because joy, as C. S. Lewis says, is the serious business of heaven.

Our task now is to trust the process and cooperate with it. We are invited to live with the rich awareness that we are always being loved by God, that God is working steadily for our good through all the situations and experiences of our lives. We must pray to accept and trust that God takes all the initiatives necessary for us to reach the fullness of our destiny and then allow our lives be a loving response. By living thus we become like God.

Again you are invited to read your story from this perspective.

For Prayer

* There will be times when you sit with Jesus and life is dark and heavy: choices that you made lovingly and carefully may seem to have no value now.

* Sit very quietly for a while. Picture Jesus turning and looking on you kindly. Hear him say: 'When you look back, remember the love that brought you to your choices. The love is what I see: it's eternal and part of God's love. An act of love affects the whole world, even if nobody sees, and it affects you too. I found this to be true so often in my own life.'

* Nothing done in love is ever wasted (Gal 6:9).

For Pondering

Notice some of your weaknesses, your neediness. Does grace come through the cracks?

Chapter Twelve

God Is On Our Side

On a dark night in January 1976, at the height of the troubles in Northern Ireland, a minibus of workers was stopped by masked men. All were ordered out and lined up. One of the masked executioners spoke: 'Any Catholics among you, step out here.' There was only one. The presumption was that the killers were Protestant.

Standing Together

It was a terrible moment for the Catholic, caught between dread and witness, but he did make a motion to step forward. Then, in that split second of decision, he felt the hand of the Protestant worker next to him take his hand and squeeze it in a signal that said, 'No, don't move; we'll not betray you. Nobody need know what faith you belong to.' All in vain, however, for the man stepped out of the line. But instead of finding a gun at his head, he was thrown backward as the gunmen, members of the I.R.A., opened fire on the nine others.

For Another

This story from Seamus Heaney has many meanings.
Here I simply want to emphasise what it means for a
person to be FOR another person. The Protestant
worker was for his Catholic friend: he showed it in
the simplest possible way, by the squeeze of a hand
just before he died. Surely the Catholic will remember that touch until the end of his life. He in turn
showed that he was for God by stepping forward and
acknowledging his faith.

To be for another person can involve one's whole
life: it can be a life commitment. It can also, as Jesus
knew, mean death: 'People can have no greater love
than to lay down their lives for their friends' (Jn
15:13).

God is For Us

I know no better statement of what grace is about
than the simple phrase, 'God is for us' (Rom 8:31).
God is for us as the Protestant worker in our story
was for his Catholic friend. God is `on our side',
working to meet our deepest needs and our smallest
needs as well. God has an unwavering positive
regard for us. Endlessly kind to us, the Three Divine
Persons accept us just as we are at every moment of
our existence, and invite us to move forward, hand-
in-hand with Themselves, towards the fullness of
life.

It's WHO you know!

We often hear it said in Ireland: 'It doesn't matter what you know, it's WHO you know that counts!' We have an instinct that to be well-connected, to be linked with important people, is very valuable. Our family had an ancient aunt who knew more about our family tree than the rest of us, and who delighted in pointing out the connections, real or illusory, with 'the people who matter'. As Christians we know with certainty what many other people would love to know, that the Authors of this universe are totally for us: we're well connected!

The incarnation provides the first proof of this: when the necessity for 'intervention' became apparent, surely it was that Jesus asked to be 'sent' and that the Father agreed out of love - Their love - for us all? The incarnation is a statement of Their total commitment to humankind. Next, the passion shows that no matter what we do, God is still for us. The resurrection provides the clinching argument that God is for Jesus and for us as his brothers and sisters, eternally. The Holy Spirit, well-described as the 'final mood of God', is now lovingly carrying the whole divine project through to its glorious completion. These truths can bring us joy and hope. God is doing all that is needed 'for us and for our salvation' so as to gather us all into eternal joy.

In earlier chapters we spoke about grace at the limits: God continues to work in our hearts even after death, persuading us to return home. We stressed the belief that God has already passed judgement in our favour, and that final judgement will be the ultimate revelation of how totally God is on our side, and how magnificently God achieves the salvation of us all.

Escorts of Grace

Throughout these chapters, we've emphasised the connection between our personal relationship with God and our relationship with one another. God is totally for me and also for you: God is for your friends and mine. But more, God is for our`enemies' - for those who haven't a place in our hearts or who are against us. God wants all other people to be for you: many are, otherwise which of us could survive?

God also wants us to be for all others. We are to be neighbours for whoever comes our way. We are to be like God for others: helpful in whatever way we can be, enabling them to grow and to be at their best. God needs each of us to be an escort of grace to all who are sent across our paths. Try reading your life story from the vantage point of yourself as an escort of grace to others.

Imagine....

Imagine what life would be like if people were truly escorts of grace to one another! But this is God's dream. Everyone would find themselves caught up in a web of support and concern rather than feeling isolated and solitary and having to go it alone. People would feel wanted instead of rejected and would have a healthy self-esteem.

Human relationships would be transformed because people would stand on the firm foundation of knowing that each is loved. To be unaware of the fact that you are totally loved by God JUST AS YOU ARE would be to miss the most amazing truth about yourself. When you do know it, there arises an urgency to share the love that is in you in whatever ways open up for you.

What about the Unloved?

To risk trusting that you are loved is the initial baby-step into the vast world of grace. Many people find that they have not been loved by those who should love them: some of God's escorts of grace lost their way or forgot the message which God had asked them to carry to such people. But we may firmly believe that God sends other escorts of grace in their place.

Even the most abandoned people can find some-one who is simply FOR them: what matters then is that they accept the love which is offered them rather than lament the absence of the love they should have had. Grace is strong and resourceful and never gives up. There is quite simply nobody in the whole world who has no one for them: the Three Divine Persons are for them, and They send others to reveal this in simple human ways. They also inspire us to pray for the forgotten and abandoned of the world.

Contemplatives have always answered this call. Thus whether they know it or not, everyone is held by love. No one can truly say, 'Nobody loves me.'

'Do they know We're FOR them?'

As Christians we often gather to celebrate. What are we meant to be celebrating? Let us for a moment imagine the Three Divine Persons, 2,000 years ago, sitting together, chatting. The world looked sad and serious, quite unlike the dream They had for humankind. People seemed lost and confused; many had turned selfish and aggressive, perhaps because they had no worthwhile dream to sustain them. 'Do they know We're for them?' asked the Father. 'I don't think so', answered the Son. They both looked toward the Spirit for a good idea. It came. The Son suddenly said: 'Let me join them: this will show them that God is on their side, God is for them!' All agreed that this was a great plan. Then They had to work out the details: what better way to be for human beings than to be born the very same way that they are? And you know the rest of the story ...

So we celebrate rightly when we catch on to the fact that the Son is THE escort of God's grace: he is the living witness that God is totally for us and is calling us endlessly into God's own happiness.

For Prayer

*   Join the Three Divine Persons as they chat with loving concern about our world. Sit and listen and allow your heart to dream with Them.

*   Watch as They invite Mary to become an escort of grace ... and then Joseph ... and then others ... and others ... and then yourself!

For Pondering

Looking back on lonely times, can you now see in some way that the Three Divine Persons were with you even then?

Postscript

All that we have said thus far is only a beginning. We have been exploring the outlines of a mystery story of incredible richness which rewards every effort we make to engage with it. Hopefully, you have found that your graced story is well underway and that you now know more clearly the mind of your co-author so that you can construct future chapters together with God.

It's an exciting adventure, and all the more so if you can work at it as part of a group. Each member then becomes an escort of grace to the others.

Dare to Trust God!

Grace is not something to be proven but to be trusted, since it's all about relationships. If you want to develop a human relationship you eventually have to entrust yourself to the goodness of the other person. It's the same with God. Can we dare to trust God? We can spend much of our lives wondering about this.

It can come as a shock to see that it is God who takes the initiative and the risk in building trust with us. The Three Divine Persons entrust so much to us. Firstly, the marvellous gift of creation, though we receive it with clumsy hands. Next, They entrust us with each other: we are fragile but wonderful works of art, and though we disfigure one another through our insensitivity, They continue to risk us into each other's hands.

Finally, They entrust themselves to us by revealing to us their dreams and by inviting us to share in their happiness. Although we betrayed Their trust by dealing disgracefully with God's Son, the Three don't waver in their loving attitude towards us.

God, then, trusts us first: we are invited to respond with similar trust. Plato spoke more wisely than he knew in asserting that life is a risk, but a beautiful risk. God has a single intention for us all, whether we know it or not. That intention is to gather up all human life into divine life: for God, this is a risk. For us to respond to it is also a risk, but a beautiful risk.

Grace is the code word for what God intends and does for us. Divine activity pervades all the details of our lives to bring these intentions to a glorious completion.

Each of us is the beloved of God. Our role is first to accept that we are infinitely loved and then to live out our lives as escorts of grace to each other.

Costly Love Wins

Only costly love will win over the world. That is the message of the New Testament. Costly love often seems wasted, but St Paul urges us not to despair of doing good: we will reap at harvest time (Gal 6:9)! 'Love never ends' (1 Cor 13:8); it is never wasted, even if it has to go underground, to achieve its task under cover of darkness.

We rightly dare to hope that grace, love-in-action, will win through at the End. Then we will be glad beyond belief that we risked loving as we did. For at the End the Father will dance, and all of us, please God, with him. Then we will all be transformed and at our best, some of us perhaps hardly recognisable! We will celebrate together in a glorified creation the sacred mystery of what God, with our help, has achieved. Then we shall dance and sing, laugh and cry with joy, love and be loved endlessly. So be it. Amen.

And so to work, to help make it happen ...